TEEN MENTAL HEALTH™

dating violence

Henrietta M. Lily

ROSEN
PUBLISHING®

New York

Published in 2012 by The Rosen Publishing Group, Inc.
29 East 21st Street, New York, NY 10010

First Edition

Library of Congress Cataloging-in-Publication Data

Lily, Henrietta M.
Dating violence / Henrietta M. Lily.—1st ed.
    p. cm.—(Teen mental health)
Includes bibliographical references and index.
ISBN 978-1-4488-4589-7 (library binding)
1. Dating violence. 2. Interpersonal relations. 3. Man-woman relationships. I. Title.
HQ801.83.L55 2012
362.88—dc22

                            2011008270

Manufactured in the United States of America

CPSIA Compliance Information: Batch #S11YA: For further information, contact Rosen Publishing, New York, New York, at 1-800-237-9932.

contents

chapter one

What Is Relationship Abuse?

Y ou are thrilled to finally have a boyfriend. He's already asked you to the prom, and he even buys you gifts. But there are times when he isn't so nice. Sometimes he sulks if you don't give him the attention he wants. When you don't always do what he wants, he grabs your arm hard enough to leave a bruise. Sometimes he gets angry for no reason and calls you names. Soon after, he says he was only kidding or that he didn't mean to hurt you. You accept it because you think his behavior is typical of

Treating a partner roughly during an argument is a sign of relationship abuse.

guys his age. Even friends think that he gets out of hand sometimes, but they still like him. You tell yourself that every relationship has its ups and downs.

Sixteen-year-old Nelly Casas wanted to be honest with her boyfriend, Jose Luis Cantu. She told him that she was interested in seeing another boy. She asked Jose to come over to her house so that she could talk to him about everything. After she told him the news, he went into a rage and strangled her to death with a metal wire and locked her in the shed behind her house. Now Cantu is in jail. He claims that he loved Nelly.

Unfortunately, this is a true story. If you are in a relationship and are afraid of your partner's anger, you are in an abusive relationship. It is upsetting to think that while you are dating you have to be alert for signs of abuse. Most people want a fairy-tale relationship—one that is perfect and free of problems, where there will be a happy ending, just like in the movies. In reality, relationships are a tangle of experiences.

Sadly, abusive behaviors are common among young people in romantic relationships. According to the U.S. Department of Justice, women between the ages of sixteen and twenty-four are the victims of relationship violence more than any other group. However, all people in relationships can become victims of abuse no matter their gender, age, sexual orientation, cultural background, religion, or economic status. This book focuses on abuse in dating relationships, the risk factors and symptoms associated with it, and ways in which you can seek help for yourself or someone you know.

Forms of Abuse

Relationship abuse can take various forms, including emotional, physical, and sexual abuse. Emotional abuse—such as ridiculing a person, calling him or her names, and/or undermining his or her self-esteem—can impair that person's mental health or social development. Emotional abuse also includes making verbal threats, constantly criticizing, and yelling excessively.

Physical abuse causes intentional harm or bodily injury to another person. Obviously, physical abuse can take many forms. Examples include hitting or punching with hands or an object, slapping, kicking, or pushing a person against a wall. Even forced playing, such as holding another person down and tickling or touching, can be considered abusive if it is done against a person's will.

Yet another form of abuse is sexual in nature. For instance, any sex act between an adult and a minor (a person under the age of eighteen) is considered abusive, even if it is consensual. Date rape or acquaintance rape, in which one person forces sex on another during or following a social meeting, is another form of sexual abuse. Both men and women can be victims of sexual abuse by their friends, romantic partners, or even family members. Strangers can also inflict sexual abuse on another person.

What Is Dating Violence?

Dating violence is any intentional attack—physical or psychological—that is initiated by a boyfriend, girlfriend, or romantic interest. According to the Texas Council on Family Violence, dating violence is "a pattern of behavior used by an individual to maintain control over his or her dating partner." According to statistics published by the U.S. Department of Justice in late 2008, one in ten teens were involved in a physically abusive relationship in the past year. Two to three in ten teens were involved in an emotionally abusive relationship in the past year.

Physical abuse is the use of force in order to cause fear or injury. Violence causes both physical and emotional harm and, unfortunately, tends to escalate over time.

Dating violence can display itself in many ways—it doesn't have to be a slap or a punch. Your partner could manipulate you into doing things you do not want to do (like having sex, for instance) or constantly tell you that you are stupid, ugly, or fat. The violent behavior can be abrupt. He or she may suddenly explode in anger for no reason. Many times, however, the violence happens when tensions are high, possibly during an argument that gets out of control. Perhaps you just said something that really hurt your partner, so it seems as if he or she had a reason for his or her response. But does that make it OK?

Think about it: even though it may have happened only once, the person you love has been abusive toward you. Also, considering that 70 percent of serious injuries and deaths occur when an abused person is trying to leave or has already left a relationship, violent tendencies are a

8

serious matter. You need to be exceptionally careful when dealing with a person who has violent tendencies.

It is never OK for anyone to hit or slap you, whether it is your parent, friend, boyfriend, or girlfriend. It doesn't matter if he or she is having a rough day or is drinking or using drugs and gets out of control. None of these are a reason or an excuse.

Violence should never happen. This is why physical abuse is defined as any behavior that purposely inflicts harm on a person. If someone shoves you, pulls your hair, bites you, or even throws an object at you, he or she is physically abusing you.

In the beginning, dating violence may take the form of "play" fighting, such as wrestling that gets a little too rough, pinching, or even holding a person down and tickling him or her. Even a little playful punching can be a sign that a person may have abusive tendencies. Other physical abuse can take the form of yanking a handful of hair, slapping the face, or pushing someone.

If a person isn't confronted about his or her abusive tendencies, or if the abused person doesn't leave, the situation can get worse. The abusive tendencies can turn into:

- Pushing or throwing someone across a room, down stairs, or against a wall.
- Burning the person with something, like a cigarette or a car cigarette lighter.
- Choking.
- Striking someone with an object.
- Holding someone down against his or her will.

Sometimes no physical marks are left after a violent scene. Maybe one person grabs another and drags him or her someplace he or she doesn't want to go. Maybe your boyfriend or girlfriend pushes you down and won't let you up until you promise never to talk to another boy or girl again. It doesn't matter whether the victim ends up in the hospital or doctor's office or not. If a person uses physical force—no matter how minor it seems—it is considered abusive.

Emotional and Verbal Abuse

Emotional abuse is any behavior intended to cause psychological or emotional distress. This kind of abuse often comes in the form of verbal attacks, or causing harm with words. If someone calls you names, criticizes you, ignores you, humiliates you, or yells at you, you are being verbally assaulted. Verbal attacks may not cause bruises, but they quickly lower your self-esteem and make you feel worthless. Emotional abuse can also come in the form of threats, unreasonable jealousy, possessiveness, or isolation of someone from friends and family.

A violent relationship usually begins with emotional abuse, or actions that cause fear in another person and makes him or her feel powerless. Some examples of emotional abuse in a dating relationship may include:

- Driving a car recklessly to scare the person.
- Going through personal belongings without permission.

- Not respecting the person's privacy; reading private messages, journals, or e-mails.
- Destroying things that are important to the person.
- Criticizing one's partner, especially in front of others.
- Not allowing him or her to spend time with other people, including friends and family.
- Constantly telling the person how to act and speak.

Emotional abuse often involves explosions of anger, including screaming at, insulting, threatening, or swearing at a partner.

All of these actions are considered abusive. They can destroy a person's self-esteem. Losing friends and family is the same as losing a support system, which can make a person feel extremely alone and vulnerable. If a girl is constantly told in words and actions that she is ugly or stupid, she begins to believe it. If a boy is repeatedly told he is a worthless loser, he will begin to give up.

The Bottom Line

Abuse is never OK. It is wrong, and it is illegal. Whatever the reason, it is not right for people in a relationship to hurt each other with harassing words, actions, physical force, or sex. It makes no difference whether the abuser is unhappy, stressed out, drunk, or on drugs. His or her abuse is never justifiable. Abuse should not be tolerated, ignored, or brushed aside. There may be apologies, but once someone uses abuse and gets away with it, it will happen again and again if the abuser isn't made to seek help or if the victim doesn't leave the relationship.

All abusive situations must come to an end before any healing can begin. However, many people find it difficult and frightening to stand up to an abuser. The first step is recognizing that there is a problem and getting the necessary help to stop it. This can be challenging because many people have a hard time admitting the abusive situation even exists.

This book will help you understand the differences between healthy and abusive relationships. It will also offer some ways in which to safely confront your abuser, get help when you need it, and assist others who may be in similar circumstances. You should take physical, emotional, and sexual abuse seriously and immediately inform a parent or trusted adult of the problem. Please see the "For More Information" section of this book for emergency hotlines and additional sources of help.

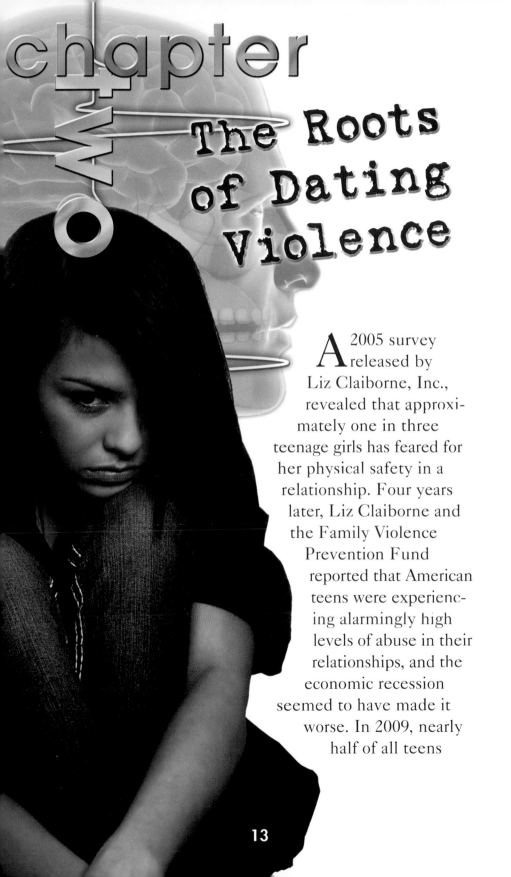

chapter two

The Roots of Dating Violence

A 2005 survey released by Liz Claiborne, Inc., revealed that approximately one in three teenage girls has feared for her physical safety in a relationship. Four years later, Liz Claiborne and the Family Violence Prevention Fund reported that American teens were experiencing alarmingly high levels of abuse in their relationships, and the economic recession seemed to have made it worse. In 2009, nearly half of all teens whose families experienced economic problems in the past year said that they had witnessed their parents abusing each other. They also reported a higher level of violence in their own dating relationships. The 2009 study provided significant evidence that today's teens are not only victims of dating violence but are also accepting it as normal. Nearly one in three teens reported threats of verbal, sexual, or physical abuse. Nearly one in two reported being controlled, threatened, and pressured to do things they did not want to do. Nearly one in four reported being victimized by distressing e-mails or text messages.

As for parents, nearly two-thirds (63 percent) of those surveyed stated that dating violence was not a problem for their teens—but the data proves otherwise. These statistics tell a scary tale. Dating violence is a very big problem. Psychologists and sociologists are now studying the reasons why dating violence is increasing.

A Culture of Violence

As teens are increasingly overwhelmed with adult issues at younger ages, they are also under increased stress. Parents and teens are becoming more isolated from one another. Add in the extreme violence that is shown on television and in movies, and the problem with violence becomes clearer.

It is a major concern that violence in the media may be contributing to the increase in violent behavior among teens. Video games, television shows, and movies demonstrate brutal fight scenes and arguments. So-called "reality" TV shows accentuate conflict and violence in order to increase ratings. While viewers are often interested in scenes that highlight lack of self-control, people rarely realize that even the reality programs have scripts to follow.

When we see a lot of violence on television or in the movies, we become desensitized to it. We forget that violence is real. When people are abused, they suffer more than broken bones, burns, blackened eyes, and bruises. Physical violence marks a person emotionally as well as physically.

According to the American Academy of Pediatrics, exposure to media violence is associated with a variety of mental health problems for youth, including desensitization to violence, depression, aggression, and fear.

The Abused Can Become the Abuser

Sometimes the physical, emotional, or sexual abuse inflicted on people when they are children contributes to their abusive tendencies as teens and adults. Although not all children who suffer at the hands of abusive parents become abusers themselves, many never learn how to relate to other people in a healthy way.

As more research is conducted, it is becoming clearer that a child who grows up in a violent home does not walk away unaffected. According to the U.S. Department of Health and Human Services, between 3.3 and 10 million children grow up witnessing domestic violence in their homes. A 2010 study led by the University of New Hampshire Crimes Against Children Research Center found that children exposed to domestic violence are at great risk of being abused themselves. In fact, the study found that 57 percent of children in homes with domestic violence were also victims of abuse.

When children grow up in an abusive household, they do not learn how to deal with their anger. Instead, they gain a very warped perception of the role of men and women in the family. These perceptions are then carried

Teens from violent homes have a greater risk of engaging in abusive relationships, according to a report from the National Center for Children in Poverty.

into the child's teen years and into his or her adult life. When dating, all of these issues begin to surface. If the abused child has not gotten help, he or she may not know how to develop a healthy relationship. Without the ability to cope with anger—and with the memories of how the parents coped—a teen raised in an abusive household can slip into abusive patterns.

People who were abused as children may be controlling or insecure. They may want to keep a partner isolated from everyone because they fear being abandoned. Children who witness or are victims of domestic violence may become overly hostile and aggressive as they get older. Family counseling, individual psychotherapy, and support groups can help break this ongoing cycle of abuse.

Organizations such as Project PAVE (Promoting Alternatives to Violence Through Education) are also working on this issue. Since 1985, Project PAVE has counseled teens, teaching them that violence is not the answer to problems, even though it may be the only solution they know. If you think that you or someone you know could benefit from PAVE or a similar organization, please visit the Web site at http://www.projectpave.org.

The Role of Drugs and Alcohol

During high school and college, many teens find themselves in social situations where alcohol or drugs are available. Dating violence tends to happen more often when drugs and alcohol are involved. People under the influence are usually more emotional and have a lower level of self-control.

However, it is important to recognize that being under the influence of alcohol or drugs is not an excuse for violent behavior, although many abusers will make this claim. Aggressive tendencies are a set part of a person's behavioral response; they do not come from the substances or alcohol the person has ingested. Instead, alcohol and drugs heighten people's inability to control their actions, so they end up turning their anger against those closest to them. Saying no to drugs and alcohol is the wisest choice for teens and their partners.

Teen Pregnancy

More than 70 percent of teen mothers are involved in abusive relationships. According to the National Campaign to Prevent Teen and Unplanned Pregnancy, three in ten young women become pregnant at least once before they reach the age of twenty—for a total of about 750,000 teen pregnancies a year.

Being a mother, no matter how old you are, increases life's pressures. Women of all ages battle depression and a feeling of isolation from their husbands or boyfriends when they are pregnant. Teen mothers' responses tend to be even more intense, leaving the girls feeling vulnerable and lacking in self-respect and self-esteem. They are often uncertain about what is happening to their bodies and nervous about what they will confront in the future. On top of this, they are trying to maintain relationships with their boyfriends. Again, as tensions increase, so does the potential for violence.

MYTHS AND FACTS

Myth: Love is when two people are so crazy about each other that they can't stand to be apart.

Fact: If one partner is possessive, it doesn't show how much he or she loves the other person. It shows that the person needs someone else to make him or her feel secure. In real love, two people enjoy being together, but they can also be by themselves or enjoy outside interests and friends. If each partner in a relationship is independent, neither will tolerate outrageous circumstances, including abuse, just to sustain the relationship.

Myth: The male should be in control of a romantic relationship.

Fact: Dating relationships are not about control. They are about two people enjoying each other's company, getting to know each other better, and working out their differences. If one person feels that he or she has to be in charge, this dynamic in the relationship could develop into bossiness and eventually into abuse.

Myth: Women are never the abusers in a relationship.

Fact: Statistics show that although it is much more common for men to abuse women, women can and do abuse men. In addition, abuse occurs in some same-sex relationships. According to the Centers for Disease Control and Prevention, each year men experience 2.9 million physical assaults from intimate partners.

chapter three

What Is a Healthy Relationship?

Everyone wants to be involved in a relationship that is healthy, but do you actually know what makes a relationship healthy? Is it healthy when your boyfriend or girlfriend does everything that you ask? Is it healthy to spend all of your time together? Is it OK to argue? When you think about it, the definition of a healthy relationship may not seem so clear. This chapter discusses some elements that are needed in order to describe a dating relationship as healthy.

Relaxing, laughing, and having fun together are part of a safe and healthy relationship.

Respect and Trust

One of the most fundamental aspects of a healthy relationship is respect. This ranges from respecting your partner's body to valuing his or her ideas and opinions.

One of the trickier parts of respect is learning to understand and appreciate the differences between you and the person you are dating. There will be times when there is just no way you are going to see eye-to-eye. Acknowledging that your partner's ideas have validity can be a tough thing to do, especially if the disagreement is about something in which you believe strongly. This is when good communication skills become important.

Trust is also one of the most important factors in a relationship. Trust is accepting that your partner is telling you the truth and refraining from acting jealous and possessive. If your girlfriend tells you she is going out with her friends on Saturday night and you trust her, you won't start imagining that she is really out flirting with other guys. Many times, if people do not trust their partners, they will try to restrict their partners' activities or tag along. This is a form of control that stems from a lack of trust.

Communicating and Listening

People in every relationship will eventually disagree about something. For example, your parents might want you home at eleven when you want to come home at midnight. Or your boyfriend might tell you that he can't go to the prom because he has to work. In both situations, expressing your ideas and feelings clearly and calmly is important. Screaming at your parents isn't helpful; neither is telling your boyfriend that you think he is acting like a loser. Instead, explain to your parents why it is important that you get that extra hour out. Tell your boyfriend why it would mean so much if he could take off work for the prom.

Communication can be difficult. In the case of the absent boyfriend, you might expect him to already grasp the importance of prom night to you. But maybe he really doesn't know your feelings about it, or maybe he'll lose

It is fine to have some disagreements in a relationship, as long as you communicate respectfully and solve problems in a positive way.

his job if he takes a night off. This is why a big part of communication is listening.

Once you have explained your view of the problem, it's time for you to listen to your partner's opinion. Practice active listening skills. This means you should be alert and really paying attention to your partner. Look into his or her eyes. Remain calm. Try your best to consider your partner's viewpoint objectively, without involving your personal feelings. This allows you to hear your partner's opinion with an open mind, and you will be more apt to understand his or her side. If, for example, your boyfriend says that his father is making him work the night of the prom, see if he will talk to his father about it. But if he has to work for a good reason, it may be time for the two of you to compromise.

Making Healthy Compromises

Once you and your boyfriend or girlfriend have explained your positions, what happens if you still can't agree?

Compromising is an intricate process. As you probably know, some people tend to be stubborn; they have a hard time understanding the other person's viewpoint. When you compromise, both sides have to give a little, meaning that each person gets a little bit less than he or she wanted in order to find a solution that works for both parties. A positive compromise in the prom example could be that your boyfriend works half of his shift and then meets you at the prom. The key to compromise is realizing that your partner's needs and feelings are as important as your own.

Of course, there are some things in a relationship that one should never compromise. The following are some basic rights that everyone deserves in a dating relationship:

- You have the right to be treated with respect.
- You have the right to your privacy.
- You have the right to say no.
- You have the right to change your mind.
- You have the right to refuse sexual advances or activities.
- You have the right not to be beaten.
- You have the right not to be verbally abused.
- You have the right not to be ridiculed or made to feel guilty.
- You have the right to not be manipulated.
- You have the right to see your friends and family.

If any of these conditions are not met, you are entitled to walk away from the encounter, date, or the entire relationship. You also have the right to get help, including calling the police or 911.

With the four key ingredients—respect, trust, communication, and healthy compromise—a relationship can thrive. There are other important factors that play an important part, too, like self-respect. If you can recognize these healthy tendencies in your relationship, you are on the right track.

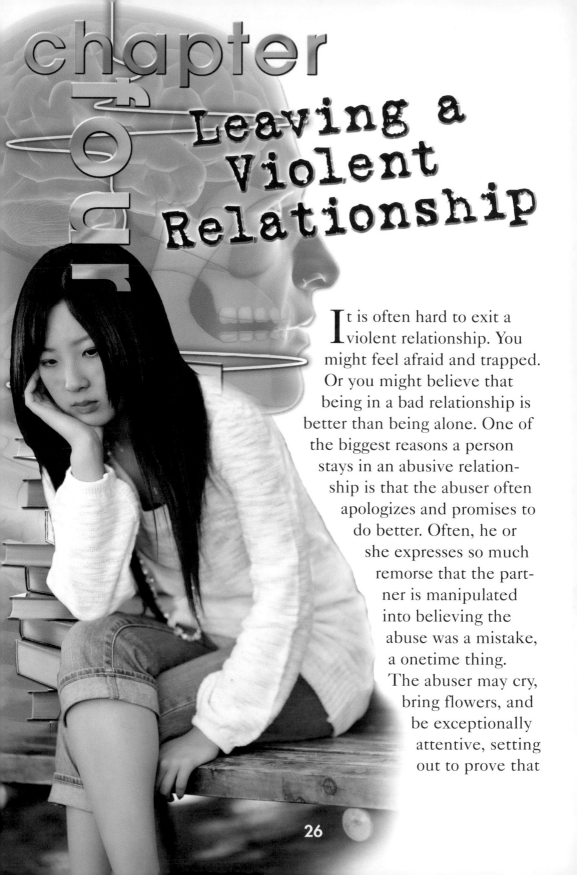

chapter four

Leaving a Violent Relationship

It is often hard to exit a violent relationship. You might feel afraid and trapped. Or you might believe that being in a bad relationship is better than being alone. One of the biggest reasons a person stays in an abusive relationship is that the abuser often apologizes and promises to do better. Often, he or she expresses so much remorse that the partner is manipulated into believing the abuse was a mistake, a onetime thing. The abuser may cry, bring flowers, and be exceptionally attentive, setting out to prove that this type of behavior is the exact opposite of who he or she is. Since the partner is in love, the victim accepts the apology, hoping that this is indeed the last time the abuse will occur.

However, an abuser is unlikely to change without serious professional help. Instead, the cycle of violence repeats itself again and again. If you think you are involved in an abusive relationship, you should immediately take steps to protect yourself. Usually this means asserting yourself, ending the relationship, and/or getting an adult to intervene on your behalf. There are many health professionals, doctors, and representatives from various organizations to help you.

Warning signs, including experiencing abusive behaviors or simply sensing that something is not quite right, should never be ignored. Trust your gut, and tell someone.

Identifying Dating Violence

Dating violence is often difficult for teens to identify when it happens in a real-life relationship. The following list of questions will help you figure out if you are in an abusive relationship. If you can answer yes to any of the questions below, you may be at risk for abuse.

- Does my partner ever hit, slap, shove, kick, or restrain me?
- Does my partner ever threaten to hurt me?
- Docs my partner call me names or insult me?
- Does my partner become jealous if I talk to other people or go places with friends?
- Does my partner make me tell him or her where I am all the time?
- Does my partner blame alcohol or drugs for becoming angry or losing control?
- Does my partner ever touch me without my permission?
- Does my partner ever force or manipulate me to have sex against my will?
- Does my partner threaten to commit suicide if I try to leave the relationship?
- Am I afraid to disagree with my partner?

In addition to answering questions like these, you can use intuition to discover the truth about your relationship. Intuition is knowing that something is not right without having concrete evidence. When someone is involved in a violent relationship, he or she may realize deep inside that something is not as it should be. Yet he or she may not pay attention to his or her intuition.

Sometimes a person starts to make excuses. No one wants to believe that he or she is involved in an abusive relationship, and it is often hard to admit when you are. It is difficult to accept that the person you fell in love with or are dating has a problem. Too often, the victims of abuse justify the violence in their minds. They may blame it on stress or on the fact that their partners are going through a hard time. For this reason, it is important to remember that there is no justification for violence. You have to think about yourself and what is good and safe for you.

If you are involved in a situation and it feels wrong to you—perhaps you do not know why—remove yourself from it because it is wrong for you. If you listen to your own judgment, whether intuitive or concrete, you will decrease your chances of becoming caught in an abusive relationship.

Tell Someone

When you have finally decided to end an unhealthy or violent relationship, how do you do it in the safest way possible? Recognizing that you are in an abusive relationship and that you need to leave is only the first step. In fact, there are a few things you should do before you remove yourself from this dangerous situation.

If you are being abused, the first thing that you need to do is tell someone. You are in danger. Your life could even be at stake. Your decision to leave needs to be shared with an adult you can trust, such as a teacher, peer counselor, family member, or religious leader.

Telling your parents what is going on is a good idea. They will know not to accept calls from the person who is harming you or let him or her visit your home. Your parents can offer you protection and get you any other help that you might need to feel better. If necessary, they can assist you in getting a protective order so that you will have legal support in keeping the abuser away.

You will need a great deal of support in the coming days and months. Leaving an abusive relationship takes an enormous amount of strength. Asking for help does not show that you are too weak to leave on your own. It shows that you are smart enough to recognize that leaving is going to be difficult.

Get Professional Help

If you are coming out of a violent or abusive relationship, you have just been through a very rough time. Have you ever heard the phrase "emotional roller coaster"? Well, you've just been riding one, and you may need help dealing with all the effects.

Being the victim of abuse can lower your self-esteem, demolish your self-respect, and make you feel worthless. A counselor, psychologist, or social worker who specializes in helping people who have been abused can help you sort through your feelings. He or she can counsel you on the healthiest and safest way to leave the relationship so that you can move on with your life. Most important, he or she can show you that the violence was not your fault.

Getting professional help does not necessarily have to cost a lot of money. Look into resources available at your school and in your community. You can also join a support group or call a crisis hotline. Some helpful sources are listed in the "For More Information" section in the back of this book.

Moving on Safely

Your first priority in leaving an abusive relationship should be staying safe. The organization Peace Over Violence offers the following safety guidelines. However, these guidelines should not take the place of talking to a helpful adult about the abuse.

Safety When Breaking Up
- Break up with your partner in a public place at a time when other people are around.
- Tell other people that you plan to break up with your partner, and tell them where you will be.
- Arrange to call a friend or a counselor after you talk with your partner so that you can talk about what happened.
- If necessary, ask a trusted friend or adult to be nearby.

Safety at School
- Always keep change with you or carry a cell phone so that you can make phone calls.
- Try not to be alone.
- Tell teachers, administrators, counselors, coaches, or security guards what is happening so that they can help you stay safe.

When recovering from an abusive relationship, lean on family, friends, or others who make you feel both safe and supported.

- Change your routine. Don't always come to school the same way or arrive at the same time.
- Consider rearranging your class schedule.

Safety at Home
- Tell your parents or other family members what is happening.
- Try not to be alone at home.
- Make a list of phone numbers. Included on this list should be emergency numbers like 911, as well as supportive people you can call when you are upset.

- If you are home alone, make sure the doors are locked and the windows are secure.

Throughout the process, stay in touch with your friends and stay involved in activities that you enjoy. Do not stop doing things that make you feel good about yourself. In addition, taking a self-defense class may give you some practical tips and help you feel more confident.

10 Great Questions to Ask a Counselor

1. What should I look for in a healthy dating relationship?

2. How can my partner and I work through disagreements in a healthy way?

3. How can I tell if my relationship is becoming violent or abusive?

4. How can I set boundaries with a dating partner, sexually and in other ways?

5. How can I reduce my risk of being in a dangerous dating situation?

6. My dating partner comes from an abusive home. Do I need to worry that he or she will become violent toward me?

7. What can I do if I'm being abused in a dating relationship?

8. How can I leave an abusive relationship safely?

9. How can I recover from experiencing a violent relationship?

10. How can I help a friend who is experiencing dating violence?

chapter five

Helping Others

One of the most difficult situations is discovering that a friend you care about is in a violent or abusive relationship. This chapter will discuss how you can approach a friend who is involved in an abusive relationship. It will also discuss some of the things you can do to stop dating violence in your peer group and community.

Dr. Connie Mitchell, an expert on violence and abuse, shows a button that she often wore as a physician on duty in the emergency room.

Recognizing Abuse

Recognizing that a friend is in an abusive relationship may not be easy—he or she may not tell you about it. You may just have a hunch about what is happening.

There are many signs and symptoms of abuse. However, keep in mind that even though a person may exhibit some of these symptoms, he or she may not be involved in an abusive situation. Knowing how to recognize these symptoms will help alert you or an adult to the possibility of an abusive situation. It is usually up to a teacher, mental health professional, police officer, or judge to determine if a relationship is abusive or not.

One of the biggest signs that someone is involved in an abusive relationship is the presence of bruises, scrapes, or welts on his or her body. If you ask your friend what caused these injuries and he or she gives vague, or unclear, answers, you may have cause for concern.

Another sign is a dramatic change in a friend's behavior, attitude, or appearance. People who have been or are being abused often keep themselves isolated from friends and family members in an attempt to hide their situation. They may cancel plans to get together and avoid discussing their personal lives.

The attitude of abuse victims can be similar to that of someone suffering from depression. Teens who are being abused might experience a decline in school performance, and they may lose interest in activities that once gave them pleasure. They might avoid social activities or have trouble focusing on schoolwork or educational goals. The following checklist includes many common, acute symptoms experienced by people in abusive situations:

- Loss of appetite
- Frequent headaches
- General nervousness

- Weight loss and/or gain
- Eating disorders
- Depression
- Exhaustion
- Self-blame
- Confusion and/or fear
- Guilt
- Shame and/or low self-esteem
- Injuries (bruises, scratches, broken bones, blackened eyes)

For instance, if your friend used to be friendly and outgoing but, since he or she got into this relationship, has been acting withdrawn and depressed, your friend may need help.

Finally, observe your friend with the dating partner. How does your friend's partner treat him or her? Does the partner try to control your friend's every move? Do you see the two of them arguing a lot? Does the partner get really out of control? If you can answer yes to a few of these questions, you should at least talk to your friend about what you have noticed.

Approaching Your Friend

The most important thing you can do when talking with your friend is to be supportive. You should not attack him or her for getting involved in the abusive relationship. You need to approach this subject with extreme care and sensitivity.

Talk with your friend. Tell him or her what you have been seeing, and ask how he or she feels about it. If your friend denies there is a problem, but you still think there is one, you may need to go to an adult for help without your friend's permission. Although you might feel bad, in reality you are being the best friend he or she could have. On the other hand, if your friend does open up and tells you that he or she is in an abusive relationship, stress to him or her how important it is to seek help and end the relationship.

Be sure to offer your support, but make it clear that you think this situation is a serious one and that an adult does need to be told. Perhaps if your friend does not want to tell someone alone, you can go with him or her. Above all, the best thing you can do for your friend is to be there for him or her during this tough time.

Increasing Awareness

Making people aware of dating violence is one of the first steps toward reducing it.

First, learn more about the topic with your peers. To kick off a group discussion, read books or do Internet research about the subject. Rent or borrow films that show people's experiences in abusive relationships.

Then share what you have learned. For example, you can put up posters in your school and throughout your neighborhood that highlight the causes and warning signs of dating violence. Most important, list the resources that are available in your community that can offer help.

T-shirts designed by survivors of violence hang on clothes-lines at Cal State Fullerton in April 2010. The annual project raises awareness of sexual and violent crimes.

Another idea, from the Family Prevention Violence Fund, is to place safety cards in places women frequent, like gyms, restaurants, or malls. These cards give details about domestic violence and dating violence that all women and men should know. They also allow people to pick them up anonymously in case they are too embarrassed to tell someone that they are being abused.

The Centers for Disease Control and Prevention has launched a program directed at preventing abusive relationships in the United States. Targeted toward youths between the ages of eleven and fourteen, the Choose Respect program aims to teach young people about the differences between healthy and abusive relationships before they begin dating seriously. To learn more about this program, and to explore more information about teen dating violence, visit the Choose Respect Web site, http://www.chooserespect.org.

Dating violence is a subject that you will undoubtedly hear more about. As the media increase their coverage and as more organizations work toward awareness, the number of people who are involved in dating violence will decline.

abuse Any behavior that is intended to cause psychological or emotional distress.

compromise A settlement of a disagreement in which the two sides agree to accept less than they originally wanted.

cycle of violence A pattern of behavior in which a person tries to control a partner through psychological or physical acts of abuse.

desensitize To cause someone to react less or be less affected by something.

healthy relationship A partnership that has a mixture of communication, respect, trust, and compromise, and is free of abusive behavior.

intuition A natural ability to know something instinctively.

manipulate To control someone in a clever and usually unfair or selfish way.

physical abuse Any behavior that intentionally inflicts harm on a person's physical being.

possessive Showing the desire to own or dominate someone else and have all of that person's attention.

psychotherapy The treatment of mental or emotional illness by talking about one's problems.

remorse A sense of deep regret for wrongdoing.

restrain To hold someone back, especially by force.

sexual abuse Any sexual behavior that is forced, taking away a person's ability to control his or her own sexual activity.

trust The confidence that someone is reliable, good, and honest.

vulnerable Easily hurt or harmed physically, mentally, or emotionally.

Break the Cycle
5777 W. Century Boulevard, Suite 1150
Los Angeles, CA 90045
(310) 286-3383
Web site: http://www.breakthecycle.org
Break the Cycle engages, educates, and empowers young
    people to build lives and communities free from
    domestic and dating violence.

Canadian Association of Sexual Assault Centres
77 East 20th Avenue
Vancouver, BC V5V 1L7
Canada
(604) 876-2622
Web site: http://www.casac.ca
This group of Canadian sexual assault centers aims to be a
    force for social change regarding violence against women
    at the individual, institutional, and political levels.

Kids Help Phone
300-439 University Avenue
Toronto, ON M5G 1Y8
Canada
National office: (416) 586-5437
Hotline: (800) 668-6868
Web site: http://www.kidshelpphone.ca/Teens
Kids Help Phone is Canada's only toll-free, twenty-four-hour,
    bilingual and anonymous phone counseling, refer-
    ral, and Internet service for children and youth.
    Professional counselors provide immediate, caring

support to young people in urban and rural communities across the country.

LoveIsRespect.org
P.O. Box 161810
Austin, TX 78716
(866) 331-9474
Web site: http://www.loveisrespect.org
This organization's national hotline offers real-time, anonymous, one-on-one support from trained peer advocates. The National Domestic Violence Hotline, in collaboration with corporate sponsor Liz Claiborne, operates the service. The Web site offers information about the issue and toolkits for young people working to raise awareness in their schools.

National Coalition Against Domestic Violence (NCADV)
1120 Lincoln Street, Suite #1603
Denver, CO 80203
(303) 839-1852
Web site: http://www.ncadv.org
NCADV provides training, technical assistance, legislative and policy advocacy, and promotional and educational materials on domestic violence; coordinates a national collaborative effort to assist battered women in removing the physical scars of abuse; and works to raise awareness about domestic violence.

Office on Violence Against Women (OVW)
145 N Street NE, Suite 10W.121

Washington, DC 20530
(202) 307-6026
Web site: http://www.ovw.usdoj.gov
OVW, a part of the U.S. Department of Justice, provides
national leadership in developing the nation's
capacity to reduce violence against women, including domestic violence, dating violence, sexual
assault, and stalking.

Project PAVE (Promoting Alternatives to Violence
Through Education)
2051 York Street
Denver, CO 80205
(303) 322-2382
Web site: http://www.projectpave.org
The mission of Project PAVE is to empower youth to end
the cycle of relationship violence. The organization's
goal is to stop the generational cycle of relationship
violence through prevention, education, and early
intervention.

Rape, Abuse & Incest National Network (RAINN)
2000 L Street NW, Suite 406
Washington, DC 20036
(202) 544-3064
Hotline: (800) 656-HOPE [4673]
Web site: http://www.rainn.org
RAINN is the nation's largest anti-sexual assault
organization. It operates both telephone and online
sexual assault hotlines with free, confidential

services; educates the public about sexual assault;
and leads national efforts to prevent sexual assault,
improve services to victims, and ensure that rapists
are brought to justice.

Web Sites

Due to the changing nature of Internet links, Rosen
Publishing has developed an online list of Web sites
related to the subject of this book. This site is updated
regularly. Please use this link to access the list:

http://www.rosenlinks.com/tmh/vio

for further reading

Baish, Vanessa. *Frequently Asked Questions About Dating.* New York, NY: Rosen Publishing Group, 2007.

Beckman, Wendy Hart. *Dating, Relationships, and Sexuality: What Teens Should Know* (Issues in Focus Today). Berkeley Heights, NJ: Enslow, 2006.

Dessen, Sarah. *Dreamland.* New York, NY: Speak, 2004.

Gordon, Sherri Mabry. *Beyond Bruises: The Truth About Teens and Abuse* (Issues in Focus Today). Berkeley Heights, NJ: Enslow, 2009.

Gunton, Sharon. *Date and Acquaintance Rape* (Social Issues Firsthand). Detroit, MI: Greenhaven Press/Gale Cengage Learning, 2009.

Haley, John, Wendy Stein, and Heath Dingwell. *The Truth About Abuse* (Truth About Series). New York, NY: Facts On File, 2010.

Lawton, Sandra Augustyn. *Abuse and Violence Information for Teens* (Teen Health Series). Detroit, MI: Omnigraphics, 2008.

Levy, Barrie. *In Love and in Danger: A Teen's Guide to Breaking Free of Abusive Relationships.* Emeryville, CA: Seal Press, 2006.

Schraff, Ann E. *Dark Secrets* (Urban Underground). Costa Mesa, CA: Saddleback Educational Publishing, 2011.

Shannon, Joyce Brennfleck. *Domestic Violence Sourcebook* (Health Reference Series). Detroit, MI: Omnigraphics, 2009.

Wilkins, Jessica. *Date Rape* (Straight Talk About). New York, NY: Crabtree Publishing, 2011.

About the Author

Henrietta M. Lily was pursuing a degree in physical education when she found her love for writing. Drawn to self-help and feature writing, she loves researching health topics and repositioning them in ways that make them easier to understand. She resides in Chicago with her husband and two teens, all of them being her inspiration.

Photo Credits

Designer: Nicole Russo; Editor: Andrea Sclarow;
Photo Researcher: Amy Feinberg